Stand!

Choosing to be Self-Reliant

Karen Okulicz

K-Slaw, Inc.
P.O. Box 375
Belmar, NJ 07719
www.OKULICZ.com

Published by K-Slaw, Inc.
          P.O. Box 375
          Belmar, New Jersey 07719
          www.Okulicz.com

Library of Congress Control Number: 2016912067

ISBN 978-0-9644260-3-0

Second printing, December, 2016

Printed in the United States of America

In memory of my Mother
Irene Olga Prostoff Okulicz

"To begin, begin."
William Wordsworth

Table of Contents

Introduction

Why a fourth book? To explain the reason for book four, let me give a brief review of the first three books.

After being unemployed twice in three years, I wrote "Try! A Survival Guide to Unemployment" for friends to assist them with how to set up a job search and structure their unemployment time. As I marketed the first book people would say to me, "I don't know, I can't decide what I want to do." I thought it wasn't that they couldn't decide; maybe they didn't know how to decide? Book two, "Decide! How to make any Decision" was born.

As I continued along with two books, I would observe those around me who were the happiest, calmest people and most successful in life. What did these folks have in common? It was their great Attitude!

"Attitude! For your best lived life" became book three.

In the time between book three and book four, a number of things happened. From my observation, the world in which we live has changed in some dynamic ways. There were more natural disasters. There were hurricanes, superstorms, fires, tornados, wind storms, mudslides, earthquakes, droughts, and flooding where no water had ever been. There wasn't a state of this union that missed these increased dangerous oddities in our weather. There was nowhere to run from these extreme weather patterns and the damage they created. For myself, I was evacuated twice, once for Hurricane Irene and then for Superstorm Sandy. On my block we were the lucky ones. Others only a few blocks away were not.

Financially, there were losses in the stock market that affected our 401ks, IRAs and CD returns. The money disappeared or declined severely. Savings with a good interest rate vanished. Has the money come back? For some. The theory was if you saved and invested conservatively, your money would be there for the future. We were all wrong on this one, myself included.

We had crippling terrorist occurrences such as the bombing in Oklahoma City, and our biggest change to a safe America occurred on 9/11 at our World Trade Centers. The terrorist threats continue. The war on terror is real and daily.

Public shootings increased. I could not list all the shootings, whether in schools, a work situation or public place, nor do I want to.

All above became the daily headlines. This mix of tragedies had created a change of life for all involved. Adding to these tragedies, we have our personal daily living dramas that may occur anytime, be they an illness or accident, divorce, job layoff, added caretaking responsibilities or any number of unexpected life-altering situations.

The operative phrase had become this is "our new normal."

So, how in this new normal do we keep our balance, our faith, our humor, and make our own healthy way of living? My witnessing of others and myself having to rebuild in so many ways with so many changes to our lives had made me pause and think: How do we successfully move forward? How do we build and maintain our self-reliance? This idea became book four.

How do we foster a strong self-reliance? We go back to the basics, stop the worry, don't take the bait from others, gain acceptance and adopt behavioral tools to keep our balance. We learn to adjust to this "new normal" with a strong sense of self-worth. We all know by now that without the respect and care of ourselves, we are ill-equipped to handle the daily trials, let alone the unexpected challenging ones.

Join me in moving forward to a perfect-fitting new normal, from the good to the great, from the chaos to the calm, and from the doubt to being assured. May book four offer the comfort of knowing you can build a life that fits you well at this moment under any circumstance.

Join me to *"Stand!"*

1

Keeping to the Basics

The quality of our lives is made by our daily choices. So, when we are handed obstacles that alter our lives, we get the chance to choose to crumble or stand.

Before we are faced with a crumbling or standing choice, it is best to keep up the basics to strengthen our self-reliance. Basics are foundational skills and behaviors that when done consistently, create a new best life or maintain the current great one. The basics include keeping ourselves balanced physically, mentally and with our spiritual belief system as well. Living a balanced life, what does that beget? Balance promotes peace of mind, your best health and overall great well-being. Keeping to the basics assists us to be our personal best and helps in setting us in the right direction when all seems lost. These are also called good habits.

Only we can structure the balance of what is important for our mental, physical and faithful lives—each of which we have more power over than we ever give credit to. We choose the balance by the daily behavior we practice. We know that what worked at 20 years of age does not work at 50 years old. Even what worked yesterday may not work today. We acknowledge that as things change, we are open to the flow of changes and options of new choices during these changes. Most importantly, we recognize we always have a choice.

Let me briefly explain each basic with an easy one first. I really should change that statement because within each "basic" is a challenge that may seem insurmountable for some and a breeze for another. The physical to me is the easiest to explain and easiest to recognize the benefits, yet still a challenge to maintain.

The basic of choosing to be physically healthy, of course, means to keep to a normal weight and be somewhat physically fit. I am not talking about being an Olympic runner at a size 5. However, if that is who you are and what you want, so be it. What I am saying is let us not get out of control with 40 extra pounds or never leaving the couch after 7 PM.

We all know by now it is best to keep to healthy eating, and some sort of physical activity will keep your body running at its best. OK, OK, I hear the screams of "I have limitations." "I can't start." Yes, we can start something and we can live within our limitations. It is our work to find what fits us best.

When we are physically out of balance, we will get many signals that something is wrong. We may have a headache, persistent cough, tired, nagging feeling of being unwell. What is triggering these symptoms? We pay attention and get them checked. This is not a book on giving details on health and the diagnostic tools to treat something.

The way we treat our physical body can keep our health at its best. We may keep the high blood pressure in check and many, many, many cancers or illnesses at bay with keeping physically balanced.

Being physically well, we keep our weight in check. As we lose the pounds, the weight comes off our hips, knee joints or giving the heart a break from overwork when overweight. An example, if you have high blood pressure and are overweight, if you lost enough weight your blood pressure will come down. A wonderful "cause and effect." Also, if you lose enough weight, you may be able to get off that blood pressure medication altogether. A win-win!

How wonderful it would be to lose weight and it just stays off. Really just to have lost weight is fabulous, but you have to keep it off. So we have to maintain the daily basics of burning more calories than we take in. Whatever diet plan you choose, it all comes down to burning those calories.

We symmetrically have to keep the exercise program and food program so those extra pounds don't creep back on. Easy? Let's yell in unison, "NEVER!"

Now, let us move on to the care of our mental health. We can only think of one thought at a time. Yet, we at times choose the thoughts of the day to be all about betrayal, or "what ifs" and "never have" scenarios. This behavior keeps us negative and doubtful. Negative thoughts do not promote a positive, balanced, healthy life ever. We must always remember we are what we think and what we think is what we become.

Since we control our thoughts, we can change our thoughts. Negativity is a poison. You won't take a bottle of poison and say, "I think I will take a swig of this today, all day." When we choose to no longer want to sit in the pool of unpleasant or negative thoughts, we change. Any negative thoughts will always drag us down.

How do we overcome these daily demons of possible negativity or doubt? By daily moment-to-moment practice. By adjusting our internal dialogue. We first witness and review our thoughts. When we work on the inside, it creates a more positive environment outside.

We can start by creating a positive inner dialogue...

I no longer want...

I no longer need...

I no longer promote...

I no longer join...

I am free to think the good to the great to the excellent.

If we recognize an email or phone number coming to us from a negative person, let's take our time to answer, if at all. Let it be. We don't have to answer every call or email. EVER.

We can never change another, but we can keep on alert when that nosey so-and-so calls and seemingly adds fuel to your negative thoughts. What we begin to do is to get off the phone sooner or out of the room quicker. It is always your choice of who and how you let others into your life. We cover how to handle others to keep our peace in future chapters. Again, this is a brief overview of keeping to the basics. There are so many techniques to learn to help with changing our thoughts, undoing the bad and adding the good. I couldn't list them all, as I will not list every diet ever invented. It is up to us to find what works best for ourselves.

The knowing that we may have a physical problem or that we wish to no longer dwell in the negativity is enough for this book. The recognition gets us set in the right direction to overcome bad behavior either physically or mentally.

Which brings us to faith, spirit or belief, the third basic—whatever you call your religion. Our faiths have many names, numerous structures of worship, and so many books with many different theories and disciplines. Yet, each faith provides a comfortable philosophy for your life. Feeling lost, adrift? Then go back to your religion or faith-based spiritual work. Go back to the basic prayers from your childhood or learn new ones in adulthood. Choose a new faith or way of spiritual care. Again, your choice and the choices are endless.

As with all basics, we practice. We practice when we choose the peach and not the peach pie. We practice when we try a new form of exercise. We practice when we say no and not join in an unnecessary conflict. We practice when we sign up for and attend a meditation group to calm us. We practice when we read from the religious books. We practice when we say or whisper our prayers from our faith. We practice when we live the principles of our faith. We practice, for we will never be perfect. We practice.

Keeping to the basics comes with the awareness of knowing what has worked in the past will help you in the future. We all know some simple things, like getting a good night's sleep is beneficial for facing a new day. Saying NO to things so you don't over-schedule yourself. Forgiving and moving on. Getting off the medication that is making you feel awful, not better. Socializing with people who want to socialize with you. And most important, whom you laugh with.

All basic behaviors have a cause and effect. If I do this, the outcome will be that. Over and over again. Eat the cookie or the apple? Say something negative to someone or give a compliment? A cause and effect of a weight gain or ill feelings created. Your choice.

Keeping to the basics takes patience and stick-to-it-ness and the ability to forgive yourself on the days when nothing goes well. Tomorrow always is a better day, a new chance to get it right. Be kind to yourself.

Doing the basics includes hanging in there when you want to quit. Hang in there with a commitment made, a treatment started, a class to finish or a marriage to salvage. The hanging in for the end result (sometimes not known) is being self-reliant.

We may have to dig deep to find what fits us with each basic and what is outdated and needs refreshing. This does not take money; this takes the time to change your mind. Keeping to our personal choices to create a life we want to live. Not someone else's choices but ours and ours alone. Our time should not be spent looking over there, but right here, right now. What is best for me, what do I need to be, ask for or explore?

It's a lot of work to get off 10/20 pounds. It is work to adjust our thoughts to be more positive and adapt our faith daily. Poor habits are hard to change but we are willing to choose what is needed and adjust accordingly.

Sometimes we may sit still and wait out the situation before we choose what is best for us. Don't say anything, don't do anything. Don't move. Let life flow. Sitting back gives the decisions time to sort things and have the answers reveal themselves.

This is being patient. We learn that patience is a virtue. Patience in waiting is not being a pushover or being lazy. There is a strong self-reliant strength in being patient. We adapt this belief that with patience everything will be shown and everything that needs to show up does.

Patience is fed by trust. We know our history. We know what we have overcome in the past. So we trust in being patient now.

Self-reliance is the knowledge that we may not know now why or what to do, but we will. That every problem will be answered, every solution presented in time. We are patient.

Maintaining the basics creates a direction that, when followed, brings the good to great in our path and we recognize it or them. When we begin to add and delete what is best for us, we poke the bear of change. And change will happen. Change may be uncomfortable, yet we have witnessed that change always has a reason to it. Change creates new avenues for the better or best.

In closing, never take lightly but relish the fact we get to live every day our own way. We have the choice in every moment to choose what is best for us. We choose habits that harm us or help us. We choose to be patient with ourselves and the process of keeping to the basics for a self-reliant life.

So, let us begin to gather the skills and behaviors, loading our bag of tricks with options on how to handle any current trials. We know that whatever is the challenge we are facing, we will be able to handle it.

We choose to STAND!

2

Don't Miss the Magic, Stop the Worry

As we move forward in building our personal self-reliance, we may need to clean house of some behaviors that may be familiar yet do not serve us well. Number one is worry.

The definition of worry in Webster's dictionary is "a troubled state of mind, to be anxious or uneasy." Nothing worse than a troubled mind, is there?

Magic and Worry, I write? What is magic? What I term magic is a chance meeting, that surprise phone call with an unexpected offer, being seated next to your next new friend or co-conspirator, mentor or new partner or spouse. An opportunity or miracle presents itself that will change something; this is magic. Serendipity and coincidence are magic to me.

There are two obstacles that keep us from seeing the ever-present daily miracles or the magic around us. One is worry and two is not being present. I will cover the first now and being present in the next chapter.

During a keynote titled "Don't Miss the Magic," I asked the audience, "How many in the room were born into the 'Worry Tribe'? Born into a family of worriers?" I asked for a show of hands. The hands went up. Lots of hands went up. I understood the volume of response, as I myself was born into such a tribe. Someone in our household was always worried about something.

One type of worry is worrying about what another person is doing. Worrying that someone else is doing better than you are. You think they are having more fun, more success, less stress, etc. The perception is if I had what they have, everything would be OK. This is the worry of "I'll never have" or "I'll never be." These thoughts of worry can go on and on with as many individual scenarios as there are people to think them.

Let me share some work examples of wasting my time worrying about what another person was doing. Sometimes we see that a worry issue clears immediately and sometimes an issue takes a while to clear. Eventually, every worry does clear itself. Unfortunately, we usually replace that worry with another ungrounded and unnecessary worry. This is what we are attempting to prevent. Our goal is to walk through the day recognizing we need not worry. Simple? Never!

Example one: There was a time I had lots of family stress and my work was put on a semi-hold as I juggled the family responsibilities and work. During this time I received a four-color brochure from one of my competitors. The brochure was a beautiful marketing tool. I thought, I can't compete with this. No time or resources to get something like that out to my prospects. Not once but twice I received their marketing material. I just felt rotten. I felt I was losing ground. I felt I could not keep up. The worry made me feel that I was failing.

As part of my work, I attend national workforce conferences as a speaker or vendor or both. I was attending one of these conferences. An employee of the four-color brochure company comes up to me to chat. They say, "We just did a couple of big mailings and you know what happened?" "What?" I say, thinking, here it comes. They did fantastic. They exceeded all goals. Contacts made over the moon. No, that was not what was said. They said, "Nothing. Nothing happened. Waste of money. Waste of time." Now, I was not expecting that answer. I thought, OK, what a waste of MY time worrying. How many hours did I think, "How will I ever get to creating a four-color brochure?" To learn I didn't have to create, produce and deliver such a brochure for my success was a relief. A big sigh of relief. I began not to worry what any other competitors were doing. I just had to keep doing things my own personal way. Lesson learned.

This lesson to oneself is to be comfortable with where we are and what we have. All growth and movement forward has its own timing. Stop worrying about what others are doing or going towards. We all have our own special path. We need our focus to recognize and greet that joy and success that has a perfectly timed arrival for ourselves.

So, that was an example of long-time worry. Really, those four-color brochures caused me many a sleepless night! Now for an example of a short-term worry.

It is a good idea to attend at least a seminar or conference every couple of years in your hobby or something career-related. This will keep one fresh with new ideas. You meet like-minded people and have a great opportunity to network with them.

For me that would be a writers' conference or small publisher conference. So as a much younger self, very naïve, with one book finished, I attended a national writers' conference. I chose a session on how an author should build a speaking career. OK, sounds good. The speaker comes out and she is dressed in a very expensive suit with very high heels, perfect hair. Very put together. Then two giant screens come down from the ceiling. Now we see three of her. She has the space-age headset and the music starts and then abruptly stops. She begins her lecture.

She presented a bucket of doomsday. "You new writers have to do this and never do that." "Most importantly, never use any notes," she tell us. Her list of what never to do grew longer and longer. How NOT to dress, how NOT to stand, and of course how NOT to speak. I am scribbling away, thinking, oh my, how am I ever going to be the speaker she was telling us to be? All the high-tech stuff. What's with the three screens? The room was small enough, we all could see her just fine without them. At this time I was gratefully long over wearing high heels. And no notes? Even back then I knew during any speaking engagement, you can get thrown off and just forget. You need to look at your notes. Sneak a peek at an outline to get you back on track.

I was worried, big time. How am I going to do this? So after forty minutes of every possible negative "we should not be doing," I was exhausted and WORRIED. How could I continue? Maybe a speaking career was not in my future?

There was a break. Thank God. The worry was killing me. Then the keynote speaker was up. This was the man we all came to hear. Let me say he was close to genius. He was a part of a book series that had "soup" in the titles. The man knew how to sell and market books. We waited. The room was silent. After a break from the "never-land lady," we sat still in fear of more negativity.

So what happens? The man walks out on stage, no extra screens, no music, comfortably casually dressed, of course no high heels. But the best was he was carrying four 3x5 cards. We see them. HE HAS NOTES. He who has marketing success in a zillion ways. HE HAS NOTES. My heart be still.

My worry on speaking was cleared up the moment I saw those 3x5 cards. Worry cleared in the time it took to replace the screens and have a 10-minute break between speakers. We will always be fine if we do what is best for us and not worry about what someone else is doing.

So, don't worry about what others are doing. Don't worry if you feel like you don't fit in while you are doing things your way. Maybe you just don't fit in with the present people, organization or career, or even family. Worried you may not fit in your present work? Time to take a class, volunteer at something more suited to you. Don't fit with current pals? Join a new gym or start a new hobby to meet new people. With family, set the boundaries with time on the phone, in the room or at the table. You control the amount of time spent and how. You have your own special path. Nothing is black and white. There is lots of gray to be who you are. The choice is yours.

So, we have stopped worrying about what others are doing. Next we want to handle our own self-inflicted worries. One of my favorite tools is to put a time limit on worry. I will say I will worry about this issue or issues next week. Let's say it is Monday so I will say to myself, I will worry about this on Wednesday of the following week. I will not worry now in this moment or in an hour but next Wednesday. When next Wednesday arrives, most times the last week's worries are forgotten. The answer has come to the question, a solution to the situation or a result to a problem. This technique has always worked for me and will work for you. Just try it.

What happens when you put the worry on a time limit? You are giving yourself a rest from worry. When you stay in a state of worry, you become immobilized. Without an immobilizing worry, we can get busy with getting the best solutions for what the worry was tied to. Worry just complicates the precious time you have for moving forward in the right direction. In worry you won't see your way through or recognize the help when it arrives or the answer when it is given. Bottom line: worry robs us of being present. We miss the magic.

I also have heard of people giving themselves time to worry. I will worry about this for 10 minutes and then let it go. This may work for you.

Another favorite tool is to use the visualization technique of putting worry on the shelf. What does putting worry on the shelf mean? Putting worry away means not to think about it. Use visualization to see yourself placing the worry issue in a box, taping or tying the box shut, putting the box in a closet or drawer or on a shelf, closing the lid or door and walking away. You need not spend another second on the worry. Worry will find its own resolution without you. You can put something away for a week, a year or a lifetime. You can think or even shout if you must, "I will no longer worry about this!" We will be able to handle whatever the situation is without worry.

Now, we have conquered how we will handle worry by putting a time limit on it or putting it on the shelf. All is right, all is well. Then you get the phone call from a family member or best-intentioned friend and they say, "I am so worried about you." What? Do they know something that I don't know? Did something happen I am not aware of?

Nothing has happened. It is their perspective and choice to keep the world in a constant tizzy of worry. So if this happens to you, just say as kindly as possible, "Thank you so much for worrying for me so I don't have to." I have yet to be that quick with this answer. I am usually going along just fine and this type of call comes and it rattles my perspective. I then have to gather myself and think, what was that? Why would someone call like that? It is not you, but them. They are sticking to their love of worry. Worriers love to share their long-standing anxieties and invite you into their worry den. Just think if they gave up worrying, they would have extra time to find what is best for them. Poor darlings.

When we conquer the negative behavior of worrying, we are able to see clearly the next answer or next right decision, recognizing if and when worries do arrive, we are more apt to go around them, through them, shelve them, put a time limit on them. We recognize the direction they give and proceed or just discard them completely. Using such tools, we are strengthening our self-reliance. Worry will not visit us or sit too long when we are self-reliant.

The thing about negative behaviors: they are easy. To worry is a lot easier than having to reach out to discover new ways to handle the worry. Complaining is easier than looking for a solution to the complaint. All negative behaviors are a trap to keep us from being our best presently and in the future. We will choose to move forward with better daily choices. What will harm us or what will help us? Every day we get to choose again what is best for us.

We remember nothing good ever comes from worry. No answers to any questions, no solutions to any problems. Worrying over ANY situation bears no results.

So, don't worry, you never have to.

3

Pleasantly Present

Being present comes naturally to very young children and animals. They are ever present for your attention. Of course the children grow out of this and become (hopefully) not-too-distracted adults. Our pets, however, are always waiting for us to show up in the present. So nice.

It is hard to be present when we are continually bombarded with distractions. Some are outside ourselves and some are our own internal distracting thoughts or feelings, like the aforementioned dreaded worry. Most of us are great at keeping our distractions going to have our guard up; keeping our guard up against what? Guard us against greeting the next new opportunities, maybe for the next new work or love? When we stay distracted, we continue to live a familiar pattern. Familiar can be a trap; distractions are a trap.

Our goal is to learn to be presently aware—to gain this self-awareness through paying attention. When we pay attention, we are honing our intuition, which is key to self-reliance. Through our intuition we recognize the red-flag warning signs immediately. Those feelings of "I am not comfortable with this" or "Something doesn't feel right." We don't have to pin down the reason for the feeling, but knowing something is triggering a red-flag reaction, this is intuition. Once we have this type of reaction, we then proceed with OUR own best next action.

We need to teach our children that if something does not "feel" right, don't do it. Don't get into the car, or go into a building, or stay with people who make you feel "funny" or unsafe. Pay attention to what is around you. You get a feeling to cross a street away from that dark doorway. CROSS THE STREET.

Intuition is having our own back. This is the best of being present as we traverse the world. We got the signal, saw the red flag and proceeded without doubt. We want to be clear with ourselves so that we live a life of "When in doubt, we don't." Being present assists us never to second-guess ourselves.

Now let me be clear here: any new habit, good or bad, takes time to implement and get comfortable with. We all have days that our work is not working, we physically feel out of kilter, and you get the call our parent has fallen and is not getting up. All bets are off on being calm moving through the day, as the sages will tell us to do. However, new behaviors will seep in as we learn about them and their benefits. When the time comes and you need to ignite them, they will be there at the ready. We are learning to keep a treasure chest of great self-care and coping skills; realizing, though, not everything works every day and there is no one-size-fits-all.

Some of the signals that alert us that we are not present are losing things, hurting ourselves by tripping or falling, breaking things, or just being overwhelmingly clumsy. What I call the injury or illnesses that result from being clumsy, I label it as "slow-down disease." Also, a diagnosis of unknown cause which has us spending our time and money chasing, what is the new illness? This unknown illness goes as quickly as it arrived. These types of anomalies are our bodies telling us to slow down, stop. Pay attention. If we took the time to pay attention in the first place, the said fall or illness may not have happened.

Being present gives us the opportunity of recognizing what needs to be alerted. The falling and slowing-down illnesses get us there. When a fall or illness has made us stop, we have no choice than to be present to mend. We have to slow down, be still, and recognize what is missing, what is needed to be added or deleted. The incident will give the "time" to figure out what is missing.

However, if we build in our lives to be present more often, we will have no need for the falls or slow-down diseases. We recognize when we get out of kilter and readjust ourselves. Too many late nights working, we choose to slow down on a weekend and say NO to over-scheduling. Also, say NO to going somewhere or joining in. We know when we are over-scheduled, over-committed or over-tired. Recognizing an overload in the moment helps us to say NO to the next request.

Being present, we "get" the cause and effect of our own behavior. The cause and effect of our present behaviors creates the next moment and our world of tomorrows. We are building our lives NOW with every thought and every action.

We choose the words to say wisely. We don't jump in and yell and say something really not necessary which causes another to have hurt feelings or causes a rift. Many of us live in the world of who said what to whom, which caused whom to get on the phone and tell what happened to another. Which then causes whomever to be angry with you also. Not worth it.

Being present provides self-respect to stay out of other people's business and clearly create boundaries around ours. This added behavior is a gift to ourselves for our self-care and mental health.

Many of us spend our lives with hand towels to clean up yesterday's messes and missing today's opportunities and magic. Why? We are not reeling ourselves in to be present. To honor ourselves with our own peaceful behavior. We are in control of our thoughts, attitude, moods, behaviors or speech.

To be present is to not make the messes in the first place, not take the bait of others (next chapter) to draw us into more messes. Being present, we act as an overseer of feelings and actions.

Being present will make you a great observer. Being present, you watch others and let them be. Not easy. Being an observer, we recognize our own behavior and those we find "trying" to be around. We observe how the "trying" ones speak to us. Do they look us in the eye? Probably not. Looking someone in the eye is very disarming to the opponent who does not have any good thoughts of you. We see them. They see that we see them and how they are behaving. They usually just back off. Try it, this works.

Being present, we feel our bodies more. What does that mean? Well, we become more in tune to what the body may be telling us. We are not letting that racing-heart feeling go by without consulting a doctor on what may be wrong. Self-awareness is the best medicine to being proactive in getting care for what ails us and leads to the treatment and cure for that ailment.

Being present, we make better decisions for ourselves. We get to a problem, issue, feeling before it becomes a full-blown challenge. We are paying attention before we become overwhelmed. We choose to think first before we make any decision. Deciding in a fast manner may not be the best for us. We stop and say, "I can't decide right now, I need some time to think about this and get back to you." Now this kind of clear behavior may really annoy another person, usually one who is controlling. You may have to repeat what you just said. "I will get back to you." Off the phone. Easy? Hardly! When we recognize that type of attempt to control us, we don't mind repeating, "I will call you!" until they get it.

So many times I would just jump in and say, "OK, I can do that," and regret that I went ahead and booked my time without thinking about the commitment. I seriously watch this with myself. Nothing worse than being stuck in someplace you don't want to be or with someone you don't care to be with. This does not make for a pleasant present.

So how do we practice this, being present? First we eliminate the known distractions. Stop moving, walking, running, driving, texting, talking, TV watching, tweeting or reading. We just stop. Be still. Listen. If your mind starts to clutter up with random thoughts, do a slow count. See the number one, see the number two in your mind's eye. This simple technique will slow you down.

Now, start counting with taking deep breaths. I breathe in for four counts and out for eight counts. Round one: in for four and out for eight. Round two, etc. Keep this up as long as you need to bring you back to focus in the moment. This is also a great stress release tool that is invisible. No one can see you do this or hear your counts. So you're called into the boss's office; start counting. This will calm you! A tool that is simple and always available and free.

As we become more present, we move more slowly. We gather the strength and the fortitude to just STOP and take a deep breath. We may add phrases: "I am here in this moment in the present." We think, I will not move so quickly to answer that next email or phone call or text or tweet or reach for that fourth chocolate cookie. We choose to be still. We are creating our own calm. We sit still or stand in stillness. Simple? NEVER.

We can silently or loudly chant a phrase or one word over and over and over. This will bring us to the present. Count breathing or breathe in with a word and out with a word. One of my favorites is, "I breathe in calm and breathe out the doubt."

We stop for the moment and in our stillness, we get the answer to what is tugging at us. Something needs to be altered, something is not right, something is unbalanced? Would the unbalance be at work, your health, relationships? Where do we have to pay attention more? What do we need?

In stillness we ask, in present stillness we listen. In the present we hear our special individual truth. There is not a religion on this earth that does not state in its scriptures, "Be Still," hear thy... Hear what? Hear our inner voice, the voice of intuition. We hear our faith. We hear our path. We WILL hear the answer to our prayers in the present.

On the flip side of being present and being still, there is "No Waiting." No waiting to be happy, thin, successful, or loved. The no waiting starts now in the present with choice. I choose to be happy, I choose to love, I choose to keep myself healthy, I choose to be ready to meet my success NOW. In the moment we make the choice. You in the moment need not to be 10 pounds thinner, or have more money or have a significant other. Right now we choose to be happy and content. The details of being, having or thinner will follow.

There are situations in life that come under the heading "Didn't see that coming." Having the skill of being present, we can stop, look, listen, observe, then react in the best way. At times the best way is simply to stop and sit still. The calmer we are, the more we will attract calmness.

Nothing happens tomorrow or within an hour that is not in process now, in this moment. If you are not present, you miss it. Miss what? Miss what it is. Miss what just happened! Miss the opportunity. Miss the gut feeling. Miss the message. Miss the love. You may miss what you have been waiting for. Easy premise to say let me be present in this moment. Very hard to accomplish on any given day, but we are going to try and keep to it. Just knowing the difference of being present or not is a step in the right direction.

This life is ever flowing, and so some days we get this better than others. However, the more we become aware of being present, it will create more peaceful moments and those moments become an hour to a day to a year. It is up to us. Can't hold on to yesterday, nor know what tomorrow brings. The present moment is the safe haven.

Since we have the greatest gift of our own self-choice, choose to find the time to be present. I guarantee you will be pleasantly surprised.

4

Don't Take the Bait

One of the benefits of living in the present, or making a conscious effort to do so, is we often will recognize a possible uncomfortable situation at its dawning. By this early sighting we get a handle on "it or them" before "it or them" blooms into an issue for ourselves. This issue may cause a physical or mental anxiety, be it a migraine or an overload of self-doubt.

One of the sightings may be those who wish to "bait us!" A "baiter" is a master manipulator getting us to say something we don't really want to say. Something we shouldn't say. We may think it but not say it. Baiters get us to say it. They get us to feel things we don't like feeling or EVER need to feel. We all have had these people in our lives.

The baiters are always around, just like energy drainers or joy robbers. Sometimes they are all wrapped in one person. Once we recognize them, we are able to best deal with their net of doom. However, the baiters are a sneaky type. They are hard to get a fix on at the start, but after we "take the bait" the first time or fiftieth time, we just want to yell, "They got me again!" I had a Gotcha moment! GEEZ!

Let me offer some examples of the craftiness of a "baiter." This is the person who slides (sneaky, right?) up next to us at a family party and says, "Why is she wearing that dress? It's too tight." "What kind of food are they serving?" Or they might say, "Did you know he and she are seeing each other?" Our ears perk up. We listen.

We don't want to take sides but say, "Well, the food is OK," said with a tone of doubt. Meanwhile, you know the food is just fine. We might then say, "The dress is a bit tight." You are alluding to the dress IS too tight. And we might add, "I didn't know he or she would date." What happened here? They got us to say or imply something negative. As simple as "The dress is tight." "Food is OK." "Him with her?" Yup, they did it again. If we agree with them or add to their negativity, they are off with this morsel to repeat to another family member at the punchbowl. We might even be in earshot when they say, "So-and-so said your dress is too tight." Who is So-and-so? So-and-so is YOU. They repeat what we just got "baited" into saying. They caught us! Now we have that headache. Did I say that? Did I mean that? We got caught with their bait. You think, how could I have been so silly to answer this person? They may get us to say something, then in a moment to months later, will use our own words against us. These "baiters" are very, very good at what they do. Experts in causing strife for others.

In the workplace they are always looking to start a rumor or keep one going. We recognize this person by witnessing their love of chaos and high drama. Baiters, interestingly, will never compliment another. No matter what a great job we have done or what we have achieved, they are silent. They do not recognize success nor happiness. Why? When someone spends their time with negative behaviors, there is no space for joy or success in their life. They are poison to themselves and others. We must stand clear of them.

I think I have allowed this type of person near me because of the need to please. Not to be rude to another. We never want to be rude or fight back with negativity with anyone. What we need to do, though, is to defuse them. Defuse any negative activity they are attempting to bait us into. We need to STOP them in their tracks.

Once we "got it" that someone is a "baiter," we now will add some tools to arm ourselves against "taking the bait." We arm ourselves with one- or few-word answers, silence or a quick shuffle, hop, step.

OK, we see them, they approach, we get ready. Plant both feet on the ground. Take a deep breath. Stand straight or sit tall, if seated. You listen. Here it comes, they are setting the trap with their latest bait. Baiting us into feeling bad about something they got us to say or feeling bad about a comment on whatever we are doing. They are a ruin to a good day. They are exhausting to be with.

OK, we now have stood or sat tall in our seats. We hear what they have to say. We don't have to answer them EVER. Don't answer them when they try to bait us to say something about someone else or company policy. This is the POWER of silence. Remember, this is a person who leaves you with a residue of hours of thinking, why would I have said that? So silence is best.

Another one of my favorite ways to disarm them is to answer with a one-word answer and walk away. The one word is "Really?" They say, "Did you hear the company is laying off in your department?" Answer, "Really?" and off you go. We can even add, "Have to go." This is the shuffle, hop, step away from them. We have just saved ourselves. Saved our company reputation or deleted involvement in family drama. Success is ours.

Don't go after them with a litany of truth, saying, "I see you and know that you are trying to poison today. I know about the untruths you weave!" They will never hear it. They are entangled in their own net. They have a strong need to always be right and have an answer to everything. If you step back and look in their garden, it usually is a visible mess. You won't find a trace of calm or happiness there.

As far as any questionable relationships, always gauge how you feel when you get off the phone or leave the person. Do you feel better or worse? Drained or clear? Exhausted or peaceful? Smiling or frowning? This will give more data to decide how much time you want to give this person in the future. An unstable person or someone up to no good will always leave you feeling a bit shaken or unclear. These feelings happen after you have spent any amount of time with them in person or over the phone, email, whatever the communication. Your time is precious and you need the calmness to care for yourself first. At times you can't put your finger on what exactly isn't right. What is it? You don't have to know. You don't have to put a label on it. Just know when your intuition is telling you something is not right. Since we are living in the present, we are picking up the red-flag signals. So, get off the phone sooner, out of the room faster. If need be, RUN.

During caretaking for my folks, I would get some "baiting statements." "Why aren't you doing, going, being, having, spending, delegating," on and on. And the ever-ready statement of "You know you have to take care of yourself." Now these people were not in my life day to day. And I would open my mouth to explain why I chose to do, have, be, deal, pay for, so and so. How I was taking care of myself and the ways I was going about it.

I had to learn to STOP and NOT answer. Most people were just trying to be helpful. They didn't really know what to say and didn't really want an answer. Sometimes I think they just were talking out loud and glad they were not in my situation. The baiters just wanted to add to any self-doubt I may have had at such a sensitive and difficult time. And with any caretaking situations, you have lots of self-doubts as you wander through the ever-changing needs of your person or people. In this uncharted territory of illness, you can doubt yourself all day 24/7. Is everything being handled in the best way possible for my person or people? Have I made the choice of the best medicine, best mode of treatment, best facility, or best doctor? On and on and on.

On the flip side of this, those who walked the path of a caretaker before me had kinder words and valid directions. They would say the doubt is normal and would never add to it. They gave trusted, experienced knowledge without prejudice. The smartest of all just listened.

We know we cannot change another person's behavior, we are only in charge of adjusting our own. So, when we get centered, any poison that is offered gets diluted to such a state that there is no effect. Watch the process of not taking the bait. It really is magical. Sometimes the person comes back and fits in our lives and sometimes never. Sometimes they are in your life due to circumstance and we get a lifetime to practice the self-care of being unapproachable. You can't fix them. People whose beliefs are rotten to them believe all is negative. It is their normal. This is NOT the normal we choose. Right! We will not add to it nor dwell in it.

We humans are fascinating creatures. Being present and listening helps us gather and discern what is best for us. If something or someone does not feel right, it is not right. I cannot repeat this enough. Once we have that "odd" feeling that another is not kind to us or a situation is not a good fit for us, we find our best way to not have it or them harm us ever.

Boldly we WILL stand strong and we smile. Not speaking but smiling. This is the wisdom of silence and the peacefulness of a smile which greatly diffuses any negativity. Life will give us so many chances to practice this stance of being centered. In fact, the energy drainer, joy robber and baiter all are tests of our resolve on how well we are treating ourselves. Just a pop quiz in the school of self-reliance, self-care, nothing more.

Today as we leave the house and are exposed to all that life has to offer, we may get the chance to practice our new way of dealing with an uncomfortable human or circumstance. We have learned to keep the baiters at bay. We stay away if we can. We need peace to live our present in a nice manner to create our best day and future.

We get to practice at the grocery store, family reunion, on the subway, at a wedding or just turning a corner. There stands the "baiter" and they approach, net in hand. What do we do? We save ourselves by standing strong, silently saying, "Don't take the bait" and SMILE.

5

Acceptance

As self-reliant champions we know we will trust ourselves that whatever is happening we will be able to accept it. We will not turn and run from the next blindside or new challenge. We are willing to continue to gather all the tools to stand, face it and handle it. We will always work towards a peaceful resolve.

Acceptance of what is allows us the presence of mind to proceed. See how things are tied together. Presence of mind, being present. You may have heard "presence" is the present to oneself. Silly wording, but true.

Acceptance means something is regarded as truth. As we view our world, we recognize our own truth. The current truth that maybe our current work is not satisfying, our relationships are not fulfilling, our life needs more joy, income, fun or love. We may have just found ourselves in an unexpected caretaking situation, accident, or lawsuit. We recognize now we have to step up to handle this new issue.

Remember, whatever we accept becomes our truth. If we say we never will be, we never will have, we never will go to, we never will finish, these thoughts create our daily reality. We accept the "nevers." We become the never-haves, the never-finishes, the never-going or never-being. It is our choice of what we accept. Simply, accept less and that is what we will settle for.

So when we accept the new issue at hand, we are able to reach out for the best assistance and ask for help. Gathering the right tools, providers of health care, lawyers, roofers, plumbers, electricians, masons, or simply finding the best bakery for unexpected company. We get it. It is up to us to make the best choice to move forward.

We reach out and we reach in. It would be so easy to quit and walk away from something when things get hard or heat up. This is non-reliant.

Also, to think that we won't get through something is also being non-reliant. There is a difference here of thinking "I will never get through this!" or thinking "How will I get through this?" Which thinking we choose will assist us in smoothing the hurdles ahead.

You may have watched others in your life walk away, not be present, unreliable, or run. This kind of pattern may have been your norm with family and friends. However, we do not have to keep repeating past patterns.

A person who runs, never sleeps well. The past or current unresolved issues continue to plague such a person. We may have had that experience. We may have let something go and not get handled. The situation never really goes away. Life will continue to give us the lesson of having to show up until we get it right. Over and over again. We don't need that and we are smarter than that. We know better now. So, stand up, cheer up and handle it. Our future welfare depends on this.

Not only do you want to stand strong, you will want those you love to stand with you. People do have many levels of commitment. Some can go the distance and others cannot. I have stood during some difficult times with people who had one foot out the door. I do not stand with those people any longer. I would make excuses: "Oh, this isn't their drama, so they don't understand the details." The reality was they were not stand-up people, or maybe they just didn't want to stand with me. If those around us are not fully equipped to join us in what is, we can let them go if we can. If you can't let them go for good, just take a break from them.

Some people are in our lives because of because. Which means they are there and not ever going away. If we happen to be loaded down with unexpected responsibilities, we can give these people simple tasks. Let them complete a task to make your life easier. They will be out of your hair. They will feel wanted and needed. A WIN-WIN, yet exhausting.

We will work to be crystal clear with our choices. We will choose not to get lost in the hurt, in the disguise of facades, in distractions that aren't working for the best. We choose that tiniest goal to conquer this moment. We know to accept our choice in this moment and our choices in the next. These thoughts help with the hand coming off the donut, cookie, piece of chocolate, not make that phone call to fuel a fight or start one. We make that appointment with the lawyer, doctor or Indian chief. This is how we do it. Moment to moment. Hateful thoughts come up; we let them go. No need to dwell in anything that is not positive.

We, of course, did not choose to be in this current "pickle." We will not let it break us, harm us, disturb us because we know we will somehow find the way to resolution. We stand strongly with our choices. We go forward now in acceptance. This moment we choose to put one foot forward and not quit. We will finish a task, no matter how small, towards the end goal of resolution, to accept the new issue at hand. We think we may not have all the answers at this time or any answer, but we WILL.

Acceptance also helps to delete the negativity of the situation. We face what may not be pleasant, but we face it. We do not waste our time with wishing things were different. We will work in this moment to make a difference. To make a possibly difficult situation less so. We do not wallow-I wish I was, I wish I had or I wish I wasn't.

Acceptance eliminates wasting energy on the thoughts of I wish I was, wish I had. Or the worst is to look over and think: Boy, aren't they lucky they don't have what I have. Waste of energy. Same waste of energy as worrying what someone else is doing. Remember there is not a human on this earth that will not have a struggle of some sort. We may never know what someone has been called upon to handle. We want to accept what we have and handle it.

We have received the call of diagnosis, the paper has been served, the storm caused the damage, you have been asked to do something, go somewhere, etc. All are equally hard times, very hard times. We don't have to like it, but we have to learn to live in the present with acceptance. Possibly gain the trust and confidence to live without what was and now accept the present. We welcome our new normal because we know only we can create what the best new normal will be for us.

If we look to our past, we see there was something that was so dire or hurtful or challenging and we conquered that. We got through it. So why the stress now over a new issue? The obstacle or pain is just re-cloaked. Most times the feelings are no different from those inspired by the last challenge. This new issue just has a new cast of characters and a change of scenery. This new challenge will also pass. We accept what is and we know, having gone through other things, we will get through the new incident.

There is no turning back when life calls you up. No place to hide or run. You don't need to fear not having an answer to the situation at hand. All that is needed is the open mind that you will conquer this, get through it or find a road around to resolution. This is being self-reliant.

Above all things, we must care for ourselves after the shock of the new challenge is absorbed. We need extra self-care for the processing of it all. Self-care is lifelong. What will work NOW to help with facing the new obstacle? One of my best healing balms is to call a friend. Possibly after a big ugly cry. A friend who has walked the walk. As I purge, they listen. As I purge, they know the depth of pain and frustration I call from. So blessed for those I can reach out to. If at this moment you do not have a trusted ally near to you, reach out for professional assistance, be it through a therapist or clergy.

What I know is as I travel through the blindsides to a new way of living, I gain knowledge. What I have gained is what I will be able to offer when I get a similar call from another.

Accepting not turning back is key in opening the doors for all answers to all problems or situations. We know that with any change, we can let it break us or let it teach us. Our choice. We show up, cheer up and handle it. To fix the hurt, to mend, to heal, to learn, to build the future. We accept and move forward, one step at a time. When we accept what is, we are able to conquer the issue and build what will be. We get it. We stand.

For all the hours I have spent in the past in pools

of worry, anguish, and hurt, I know now I could have used the time better. That's the point. We need to make our time well spent. Not to feel hurt or sit in frustration but to reach out and find the next new solution to an issue.

We know whatever the missing questions we may have, we will find the answers. We step forward in approval of our tiniest action with acceptance that there is no turning back. We accept our choices at our timing for our own peace.

6

"Just Once"

We recognize that being present is a powerful tool for self-reliance. By being present and having acceptance, we now will add the awareness that most difficult situations in our lives happen "just once." This "just once" belief may offer comfort in many, many varied and challenging times.

This is the comfort of knowing I only have to do this, go through this, put up with this, handle this, solve this, be a part of this, "just once." If I only have to go through this once, I can handle it my best way possible to the final resolution with limited anxiety. Your best way is up to you.

Top of the list of "just once" occurrences is, of course, the death of loved ones. When we are faced with the death or dying of our loved ones, the emotions and feelings are so overwhelming, they make time stand still. We can and do get lost in grief as we are witnessing our loved one's passing. We also will be lost for awhile after their passing. A loved one also includes our pets, of course.

"Just once" could also be an overwhelming debt,

lawsuit, divorce, illness, unexpected caretaking or facing a natural disaster's aftermath. I am sure you have even more examples of a "just once" scenario you have experienced. They may be the incident that triggers us to have to craft our new normal.

It seems we all are getting a taste of natural disasters, be they floods, hurricanes, earthquakes, droughts, fires or tornadoes. I cannot claim to know the devastation of losing everything to a disaster. Though I do know what it feels like NOT knowing if you have lost everything. I have been evacuated twice from my home, once for Hurricane Irene and then for Superstorm Sandy. With Irene I had no damage or power lost. For Sandy, I did not know how my home fared. When I received that phone call that said all is well, what a sigh of relief.

We could have a "just once" that comes as a betrayal at work or a love lost. There is no hiding from handling a "just once" situation. There it is, present, large and looming and must be taken care of. We may be in a position of having multiple "just once" states of affairs at the same time. We could be caretaking and lose our jobs. You can name a variety of conditions that you have lived through, or are right now living through them.

We may have bouts of illness or looking for a diagnosis to an unknown health problem. An illness that may have a long hospital stay with complicated procedures. Hopefully, "just once"!

When we think we only have to do something "just once," we can look at it with a clearer vision. It makes the unknown less ominous. We become so grateful that it is only a "just once" event. We may only have one more time to see the doctor, one more time to meet with the lawyer, make one more payment to delete the debt, make one more phone call to arrange one more visit. This does not eliminate what has to be done, but eases the mind when doing so. We know it is almost over, almost done. Our health and mental welfare depend on our perception of what is happening.

We also are offered the choice to have a "just once" define us. Some wear a tragic struggle as a badge for living and stay in the muck for longer than necessary. Others just add the situation to the life story and move forward. We may do both in the litany of life obstacles. We again have a choice in which we choose to linger or move forward. We all know people who love to stay "stuck" in a past betrayal or something tragic. It truly is easier to have something keeping one unhappy than to stand up and give ourselves the time and effort to move forward to a better place of contentment. Which do we choose?

When the "struggling juggling" time is over (and it will be), you can say, "I never have to do that again." Be at peace that you showed up and did your best. Right here I stop. For those who are doing "caretaking" or healing from something, do not be angry at those who did not show up or call or offer or stop by or send a card or just vanished. I suggest you let them be. Hard to do, letting the ones who did not show...GO. Rid your bad feelings about them from your mind, from your thoughts.

Do not pick a fight with the no-shows. No demanding questions like "Where have you been?" Better yet, "Who are you not to show up?" They know where they were and why. The ones who showed up, you honor and tell them you are grateful for their presence and assistance.

We really never know what is in store for us and we don't know what is in store for them. Sometimes we get to see the cause and effect of others' poor choices. Most times we will never know that their awful behavior caused an unhappy outcome. But know everyone has that "something," as my grandmother would say. Which means someday they will have "something" big in their life that they have to handle.

It is HOW we deal with such burdensome ordeals that builds us the life we live. We build our best life with our daily choices. A burden to one is an accepted challenge to another. Our choice. Knowing we have to do something "just once" takes the sting out of it. This way of thinking may make you more organized and determined to not go down the road of self-pity or depression. Why waste your time when something is not forever? Really, what is?

However, at the start of a "just once," there will be shock, tears and fears, anger and thoughts running amuck. What has happened that such responsibility has arrived in our lives? Soon enough we face the reality of what is. We need all the energy to make that next phone call and cannot afford to be drained by any outside influences.

I am always amazed that when I let a bad situation or person go, I am always sent a better solution or help. Why? I think acceptance of the best will draw the best. So, do not clutter your thoughts with someone else's odd behavior, the clutter of who is disappointing or hard to deal with. By doing this you are accepting less. Is this easy? Never.

On the lighter side, here is a simple example of recognizing what works and what does not in a stressful "just once." When caretaking my parents, it was at my childhood home loaded with childhood memories. One memory was of our local Italian bakery, Vaccaro's. My dad would bring home their jelly donuts as a treat. So, when visiting my folks, I would go to that bakery for a supply of jelly donuts. I ate the donuts, I ate lots of donuts. Jelly donuts with powdered sugar. Lots of them. I must say this did not work. Extra weight is never a lovely thing.

It is also our choice how WE want to be when the "just once" ends. Would we want to struggle with extra weight, which breeds frustration? Always our choice. Remember when the event is over (and it will be), we get to live a new way. How will that be? Mad? Angry? Unhealthy? Unhappy? Regretful? Your choice. I eventually throttled back on the donuts.

More than once, on driving home from a day with my parents, I had the feeling of being so overwhelmed. How will I clear the house, move my mother, handle the passing of my dad?

How? By clearing one kitchen drawer at a time or making one more phone call to set up something, or get the answer to something. To this day, when faced with what appears a large obstacle, I look at the big picture and say, "One paragraph at a time to finish the one chapter to finish this book four." You don't write a book in a day nor clear a home out in an hour. It takes discipline and tenacity and our newfound wisdom to know one step, one call moves us forward. Some days nothing gets done, but that is fine. We know that next day we get the choice of another closet or box or drawer or appointment, all in the course of moving forward to the best for ourselves.

On the other side of the coin, you may be the person who has never been "called up" yet. What does "called up" mean? In our family, when we hear that a person has had something unusual happen that they must handle as an individual, we call it "Called up!" Called up to serve another, called up to show up, called up to handle, called up to be present, called up to grow up. You got the call and you're now front and center in something, you have been "called up."

You also may have a chance to be a visitor to a sick or dying friend or loved one for the last "just once" visit. Make the visit. Do it for the person or do it for yourself. Knowing you only have to face this "just once" takes the fear, hurt or anger out of the circumstance. You only may get one chance to say goodbye or make a one-time offer to assist in some small way.

As an outsider, be kind and compassionate. The right thing to say is to ask, "What can I do?" "How can I be of help?" "What do you need that I can get you?" Tell them if they don't know today, but may think of something, please call upon you and leave your number. What a perfect world that would be! Now if you have indicators that you can't or do not have the wherewithal to help, say nothing.

In the "just once" challenges of life may be your own personal health. Gather the best care for yourself. Choose the best people to go the course with you. Sometimes the choice will be surprising. Who you thought would show up doesn't, and who you wouldn't think, does. Life is so interesting. Be open to the surprises. Kindness of others is always waiting to be accepted.

How you handle your "just once" is as individual as we all are. Don't be bothered by others trying to give you advice about things they know nothing about. Keep your time limited with those kind of people. They may be giving advice that is not the best fit for you or your person. They may call you up and tell you what should be done. You don't have to listen. Phone away from ear, let them talk. They may think by giving their view they are helping. Meanwhile you are the one with facts and figures on what is happening. Just say, "Thank you for your input" and move forward your own way. I would get angry or be hurt and think, "Don't they think I thought of that point already?" I found this was exhausting. You need to keep up your own pace and not be dragged down in a muck of bad feelings from any unnecessary advice given.

One of the hardest things is not ever knowing how long the "just once" lasts. That is why we must stay calm during this time. Anything that will keep you calm and clear to make the decisions that have to be made, you should embrace. To stay calm to move forward for the best for all involved. This, again, comes with the acceptance of what is. I accept this situation now and don't fight going through it. Being in a "just once" like caretaking or being ill is like peeling an onion with so many layers. And on the days when our "just once" situation eases up a bit, be so very grateful. Gratitude will fuel us to move forward.

So while we are going through this event, we can at times put some distance and a detached view of "just once" thinking. Keep our thinking clear by saying to ourselves, I only have to make one more move, have one more surgery or make one more decision. If I have go through one more _____ (fill in the blank) to get to the other side for a more healthy body, maybe better mobility or a new freedom to find someone better suited for us or to live in single bliss after a divorce— our choice for our new normal—the daily drudgery of daily physical therapy, FEMA details or a call to the lawyer is not fraught with so much anger but with a calm acceptance. That is our main goal: to stay calm, to stand strong. To keep our peace to make our best decisions and follow our best direction at all times. Sometimes changing the direction or decisions happens in a moment. Your view of what is happening is a gift to yourself. This gift will build your self-reliance.

And when our "just once" ends, it is up to us to remember what was helpful and then help another. We will reach out and ask and offer and mean it. We will show up if possible. If we can't, know that is also being self-reliant. Our self-reliance includes our best self-care.

To best move forward with the next new action to smooth the way, we will take a big, deep breath, knowing we only have to handle this "just once."

7

Choosing to be Better, Never Bitter

Over the years friends have suggested that I write a book on caretaking, as I have had decades of experience in many varied situations. My thoughts on this have always been, as demands increase and free time becomes limited, a caretaker does not have the time to read about the tasks at hand. Neither do they want to. I surely did not want to read about it during some of the most troubled times. I was living it.

However, I do feel it is worth mentioning caretaking, as this is a book on self-reliance. During any caretaking there may be some very important choices that must be made that come down to you alone. So you need to be able to be your most trusted ally by being as self-reliant as possible.

Caretaking can take the form of having a special needs child or ward, an ill relative, significant other, or friend. It could also be the unexpected accident or illness which has befallen you. You now are the one in the doctor's office waiting for test results and looking at an unknown path to healing.

As a caretaker you may not only have to handle another person's health care but also their housing, food, transportation and finances, as well. You become their advocate in all areas. A lot of endless details go into the care of others. Just like any difficult event, with caretaking, you really never know the length of time you will be needed or the amount of time until you will be well. If we got a message somehow that told us you will be doing this 6 months, 2 years or 10 years, whatever the time, I think we all would be better equipped to handle our duties with patience. We'd think, "I can do that." I will be able to hunker down and proceed. I'd be able to build a life around what my new responsibilities are. But that is fairy-tale thinking because as a caretaker, you awake every day to the tasks and unexpected emergencies. You begin to think, how long can this go on? We must deal daily one task at a time; with one task completed, on to the next and then the next. Slow and steady with the knowledge we don't know how long something will last or the degree to which we will be involved.

In caretaking you will also face many "I didn't see that coming" scenarios in such uncharted waters. Be it the odd letter that says a procedure is not covered and now you owe, or you may spend days or hours fixing the problem, later to find out it was a clerical error of one digit off on the medical insurance card. This happens.

Not only do you have the daily items to keep up with, you have the unexpected "I didn't see that coming" occurrences which can (and will) test the best of us. There have been times I have felt, and others in my shoes have expressed, the feelings that you feel like you are drowning, choking, suffocating, out of your league, completely overwhelmed, exhausted, put upon, claustrophobic, alone, feeling restless, confused, cornered, and just overloaded in servitude. You may feel that daily ties that bind continue to tighten.

With all these feelings to process, then you get the clueless person who wants to talk about their latest vacation plans. One could snap. But we don't snap, because the struggling feelings will pass. You fix what needs to be fixed. You find that joy shows up as you witness your person open their eyes and recognize you or take the first step after surgery. The relief when told they get the OK to return home. Therein lies the joy. Pure joy. All hassles are forgotten for the moment and we continue. Some people are not so lucky to care for those they love or even for that matter love themselves enough to take the best care of themselves. Very sad.

So, how do we handle caretaking? We handle it the same as any rug pulled out from under us. We stand straight and tall and begin by taking one breath, ask one question, take one step, make one decision, write one note and move forward. We will not break, we will bend. We add and delete what works and what does not. This may be to delete certain doctors, medications, meddling people or bad habits. We deal daily with one task at a time, complete one task, then on to the next and the next. Slow and steady.

One saving grace for me was the 70-page school notebook. Always on sale in the fall with back-to-school supplies, it was my record keeper, a log book and memory jogger. This was the success to an organized path to follow. Similar to keeping a journal of the journey, filled with details that are easily forgotten amid the chaos.

Having the notebook will keep you in check. With the notebook you chart the tale of your person. The appointment dates and what happened, what questions you need to ask. You keep the phone numbers of doctors you spoke with and post all conversations you have had. So when an insurance company rejects or misplaces something of importance, you have the date and time written down. You can't possibly remember all that needs to be done or has been done. All the cards of doctors or facilities get stapled in the notebook. It is the guide and the history. There is a comfort having all this information. Especially when you are asked for the twentieth time at an ER (Emergency Room) the same questions. You have the documentation. You don't have to second-guess your memory on dates and times; you have this in the notebook. Of course you can use a tablet or laptop or your phone to do the same.

Also, separately in a large envelope, keep copies of

medical insurance, Medicare card, prescription cards, photo ID, power of attorney, living will, DNR (do not resuscitate), any medical device card which could be a pacemaker, implant or a heart-looping monitor, limb implants, and a list of medications and allergies.

After many calls to drop and run to an unexpected ER visit for my folks, I began to add a "go bag." You get the call that your person is going to the ER, yet again. You grab the "go bag." It has the envelope with all needed documents, the notebook, plus treats, maybe a bag of nuts and chocolate, of course, reading material, bottled water and the cell phone/tablet charger. Add fresh fruit like an apple or orange. All things to keep in hand's reach for the unknown length of an ER visit and/or possible hospital admission. You will and do get good at the unexpected. Being prepared for the expected unexpected helps keep us focused and calm.

There were times when my mother wouldn't eat, and I had wonderful family and friends who would go and assist her to eat. I always made the end-of-day meal. The end of day to review with staff what happened in that day and what was her progress. One year she was in rehab or the hospital almost 100 days.

As with any struggling situation, there will be humor. After so many hospital or rehabilitation facility meals, I witnessed that carrots are the continued vegetable on the plates of such institutions. Carrots must be the cheapest to buy and the longest shelf life? I also had enough fruit cup to last a lifetime. I became fascinated with how the fruit cup pears were always cut in perfect squares. That must be some fine machinery.

Not so funny are the "others," be they family, acquaintances, friends, staff, etc. The "others" want to give you unsolicited advice. They are usually the people who have not shown up for anything. Not sat an hour in a waiting room or got the call to drop everything and go to the ER, let alone process the sight of death's arrival. In the face of these stressors who pour the unsolicited advice on us, we will be silent. We choose silence. We need our peace to focus on the main event.

You could just lose yourself and scream at these type of people, "Stop with the advice, already!" It has taken me a long time to learn to just look at them, let them spin their wheels. You will get nothing of value from them. Your plate is full and you need your energy to handle the daily needs of yourself or your person. Let them be.

Haven't you noticed that the most opinionated people usually have lived less? No adventures or being in the world. They sit and let everyone know how others should live. Interesting. We will gain comfort and value from those who walked the walk. Been in your shoes. Showed up. Stood strong. Those are the ones who know the power of listening in silence. Mentioned this before, haven't I? Well, silence is golden. A blessing of caretaking is we learn quickly what in this moment is the most important task, call, or thought to have, hold or achieve. We become the experts of on-the-spot, split-second knowing what to choose and what to let go. With this knowing we are flexible without self-doubt. We gain the knowledge that what worked yesterday may not work today. We know this and proceed accordingly. We get to examine how we are living in the present and how we want our lives to be better. We dig deep to find our joy. There will be a very strong pull to search for "joy in place." We search and we find it and we will be better for it.

I have a dear friend who took care of her mother in her home for years. She didn't get much time to be away from her home. What she did was make her front yard a beautiful garden of roses and lavender. You don't have to venture out. My friend was home, she was close to her mom, she created joy in place.

Finding your simple joy does not take money. With all the love and attention going into caretaking for another, you need to save some for yourself so that you can refresh to face the next decision or event loaded with decisions. Not sleeping or not exercising or resting is not going to help you. EVER.

This finding your joy enables you to rest and recharge. It could be reading a novel, doing puzzles, making something that gives you joy in place. You dig deep for new coping skills to face what is happening.

You may try a new gentle yoga technique or breathing exercise to use at any time or place. This is part of digging deep to find your own peace and joy. There is every type and level of free exercise or relaxing techniques on the Internet. You may begin to search for these new skills. You find what works for you! Your joy is yours and specific to your personal nature. This is a secret for yourself. No one needs to know or make a nasty judging comment that you find peace in watching reruns of some reality TV show. This may be one of your secret techniques that keep you sane. What makes you happy gives you moments of peace.

Self-care could include a prepared or take-out meal for yourself that is healthy and waiting for you when you return from the hospital or rehab visits. This is a tiny thing, but this will save on eating poorly and keeps you healthy. Maybe having a special treat of chocolate or a cookie (not the entire bag). Plan ahead with something kind and enjoyable for yourself.

What balms heal you? All this reaching out and digging deep to find what is best will stay with you when the situation is over. These new hobbies or coping skills are a positive consequence of your caretaking well done. It is your choice to find what works.

You learn what to bring with you to accomplish while waiting for your person to have their next chemo session or procedure. What hour or half-hour can you find to take a walk or sit in a park, garden, etc.? Where is your joy? All hospitals have chapels or meditation rooms. Find them. Go sit and be still and pray or just sit still and breathe deeply.

I will share one of my not-so-secret secrets. I love garage sales, estate sales and consignment shops. They make my life different and bountiful. When I find that perfect porcelain bowl for a dollar, I appreciate the treasure. Maybe I couldn't spend the morning going to a dozen sales, but I could stop at one or two and get my "bought this for a dollar" fix. Take that treasure home, clean it up and enjoy it.

Have a book or movie or magazine waiting for you when you return from a visit. Go to see or call a favorite friend. Spend a half hour weeding. Even the satisfaction of completion of cleaning out the refrigerator or junk drawer. Hitting a bucket of balls. A sauna at the gym. Long hot bath or shower. A moment of silence in prayer. Being with a grandchild or niece or nephew to be in their world. Walking the dog, playing with the cat. You create the comfort for yourself and always. Don't have to tell ANYONE what those comfort moments are. Only you know what gives YOU peace in place.

Caretaking is not a license to overindulge in snacks, alcohol or pills, or take up smoking again. You then have to undo the extra weight and bad habits when the time is over. Not worth it.

In truth, caretaking is a loss of any control of your daily day. As I look back on my earlier years of caretaking, I would get home and flop on the couch and stare into space. I couldn't think what was next. What was coming? What was the next emergency? I had to learn to take it step by step, a moment-to-moment approach to my day. Self-care became looking at the caller ID before picking the phone up or answering the text or email. What energy do you want to expend answering any or all messages? Make choices to conserve your energy in small ways, like screening your messages.

There will be times of overload when you are invited places and don't think you have the energy to go. Watch yourself. Don't bow out of everything. Attend you must, even for an hour. Get out and be a small part. Keep the connections that are important.

This finding joy and what works for you is a big part of what you are facing. You weed out who is who and what is what. You get the gift of being in "IT" with a loved one in a way that no other event would have made you closer. You are grateful to be a part of the process. This is a really hard time that does and will have an ending. You honor yourself knowing you are there for the duration. As we become self-reliant, we build the strength and fortitude and believe in our abilities to find and create the best life in the situation that is set with so many constraints.

If you know of someone who is caring for another, don't be the faker. Don't tell the person, "Oh, I'll be back," and never come back. There will be times for those people that their world is the size of a nickel going towards the size of a dime. The world of hospital, doctor appointments, therapies. Fake visitors have their own side effect, often worse than medications.

Don't be the faker who smiles and says, "Oh, I'll help you!" You never see them again. "Oh, I'll get you that item." Never to receive what they went to get. People who are ill or the caretaker are busy healing or helping. The caretaker for another or the patient most likely are not deaf and at least one of them does not have a loss of memory. Think before you offer; they may depend upon you, crossing that task off their long list. If you can't help, don't say you can; if you can't visit, call or send a card.

As caretakers the demands change on a dime and we are off handling another issue that we didn't or couldn't see coming. Plus, we may be the only one with all the details. In this instance we may answer back slower. Perfectly fine to say, "Can I get back to you? I am in the middle of something." There may not be anything pending at the moment but the need of a respite from conversation. The responsibilities may be exhausting and there is no need to explain yourself. EVER. We are practicing self-care. This is self-reliance. It may be the best to never answer back and of course never to take the bait.

However, hard as caretaking can be, we know we don't want to ignore the process. There are no do-overs with this "just once." We know the time will end. We don't like everything that is happening, but we know we don't want to miss it. We do not want to have any regrets, and by doing our best, we won't.

By moving slower, you recognize the tiniest positives and are grateful. Getting the best appointment time and when showing up, getting a great parking space make your day. Having your favorite nurse on duty. Fixing an issue simply. These details that are helpful, no matter how tiny, make us grateful. Having enough of everything on any given day makes us grateful. The small positives matter.

And when this ends, we will grieve the person, not

ever the situation. Many who read this chapter may be just starting out, having been alerted something is not right with so-and-so. That ER call just came, or the diagnosis told. You have been CALLED UP to handle another.

We make our choice now to be better, never bitter.

8

Prepare so Not to Despair

Self-reliance takes a bit of preparation. We gather the flashlights and have bottled water ready for the upcoming storms, but we need to prepare in other areas as well. We prepare both the inside as well as the outside.

We are attempting to manage any panic, hurt, and sometimes overwhelming frustrations of life by being a bit prepared so not to despair. We start now to prepare for the future. We are creating our own luck here by creating the best of everything for ourselves. Being a bit prepared daily, we are making an obtainable path towards our future success, happiness, contentment and calmness.

How we create a preparedness life is by gathering skills to live in our own personal way. What is the best for us? We all know by now exercise creates calmness, lessens stress and helps us sleep better. There is no doubt about this. Exercise works! It is the magic pill for every ailment. Again, we get to make the choice of what type is best for us.

Bad day? Take a walk, a bike ride, throw some dirt around in the garden. You are changing your inside and outside. Shrinking the stress by a run may also get some weight off. A win-win. There are all sorts of chair exercises, even chair yoga for those who have limitations. There are levels of how to be fit for everyone. It is our choice what fits for us. We make our choice and gain the benefits of a thinner self, calmer self and a good night's sleep perhaps.

Having my own business for over 20 years, I have learned to keep working when nothing "seems" to be working. Is this easy? NEVER. I can list dozens of reasons that people have given me why books aren't sold or why I wasn't chosen to do a workshop or keynote. To this day I will still get a "NO" that I never even thought of. "No, we can't buy books because our parking lot is flooded." OK, I guess?

I never stopped working when things seemed not to be working. My preparedness was to continue to prospect, go to conferences and make the follow-up calls. In fact, I would work harder at prospecting to find new areas where my books might fit. All while getting the follow-up responses of "Not now." "We have no budget." "Sorry, have to put the book order on hold."

The working when nothing is working fits for many areas of our life. Wanting to lose weight, we struggle to do our exercises and we eat a bit better and nothing seems to happen. Until the weight starts to drop off and we see and feel the cause and effect of exercise and eating smartly. The clothes fit better, we feel better. Takes time and effort.

Our social lives may have changed by the moving of a friend, death of a spouse or the children are gone. We want better or more company and we reach out. How do we find new people to spend our time with? Maybe we join a club. Turns out the club members are not a fit for us. So we reach out again and wonderfully this new club, hobby or volunteering is a fit. We are working towards a new goal when nothing seems to be working. As we work towards this goal, things fall into place and we discover a new "something" positive for ourselves.

Working on being happy has many trials also. Know that being unhappy is a trap. When we are unhappy we lose the joy in life, we maybe become angry, frustrated, maybe even lazy and never good company. It is work to be happy. Working to be happy is hard, unhappy is easy. Let me be clear here: happiness is not the "smiley face happiness" but contentment that I know that I am doing what is best, living what I want or making progress daily to continue to stay the course. Very easy to sit back and say, "Wish I could, wish I was." Harder to get out and take a class, join something to better yourself. Easy to say well, maybe I won't like the course, not for me or I might not fit with the group. So you do nothing and what changes? NOTHING!

We could play "I would have had, would have been done" if "I didn't have or I wasn't." Wasn't what? A blame game of nonsense. Right now someone is reading this and saying, "But my life is different!" (Aren't they all?) "I would have been the best if I didn't have..." OK, maybe you are not going to be the star basketball player at 4 feet 2 inches. This is true. However, we now choose not to be unhappy with our reality. We start to

BE the best of what makes us happy because we recognize our own unique ways that make us happy NOW. We find our way to happiness by reaching for the new. That is the point! If you don't reach out and try and prepare for the new, guaranteed nothing new will happen, nothing will change. The weight nor your circle of friends or income. Nothing changes or gets better until you adjust, reach out and prepare for your own successes. You work on it.

Remember we mirror our own behavior. Interesting concept and very telling. What does this mean? If you get calls from friends or family saying how everything is bad, the sky is falling mixed with "hate" talk—I hate this, I hate that—listen to yourself. Is the person mirroring what you are saying? Eye-opening with a bit of uh, I don't like it. We really must watch our words. Why be wasting our time on the phone with the haters when you could be looking at a catalog on lovely plants for the garden or planning a getaway with someone fun. Remember we will always draw to us what we need to learn or alter.

Personal or professional success begins in small ways. There seems to be a disconnect with people thinking they want to be a writer, rock star, actress, inventor, business owner, Nobel Prize winner, Oscar winner—today. They want to arrive to pick up the award or succeed without any trials, education or practice. All without gaining skills and finding what does and does not work.

All success take time, effort, practice, discipline and sacrifice. Sacrifice can be as simple as not buying the bag of chips for a future weight loss, making the commitment of taking a weekly class at night by postponing a night out with friends. Which do you choose? Be it 10 pounds off or a college degree, it will take time and due diligence. We will move forward, we will lose, gain, achieve, conquer, learn, ALWAYS our choice. What choices we make lead us to what is better for us or not.

Being self-reliant, we see the quicksand before we step in it. We do not let anger go on too long. We know we have weathered the storms and turmoil of "just once" situations and now we will put into our bag of tricks some of the tools, tricks and comforts of self-reliance to keep us sane going forward. We know not to spend too much time doubting the unknown. We know, having witnessed our past, that doubting future success did not beget current success.

We recognize that daily we get to tell the world how we want to be treated. Simple example: I had a friend who would wear very expensive suits at her entry-level position. No one knew most items came from a consignment shop. She looked like her boss's superiors. Who always got promoted? She did. She had the skills, no doubt, but she prepared her attire and dressed for her success.

How we present ourselves to the world speaks volumes of how we feel about our self-image. Do we want to shout to the world, "I don't respect myself enough to look my best"? Since I am shouting, "I sure don't respect myself by not caring about my personal appearance!" why would a company respect me to hire me to do business with them? We need to be prepared to meet the next new success. Be aware we are always being observed, especially in the workplace. Socially, who wants to be with an unkempt or ungroomed person? This does not take an expensive haircut; it may just take a comb through your hair. We are always loudly telling the world what we deserve. Being self-reliant is being self-aware. We know those fabulous comfy-couch clothes are indeed for the couch, not for the office or meeting your significant other's family.

Being self-reliant, we prepare, we practice, we learn new skills, we reach out—all to build the best next moment, hour or day. We know that when faced with a challenging time and our backs are up against a wall, we don't crumble. We take that deep breath, view the situation and slowly, so very slowly, we proceed. Proceed to find an answer, a new skill or behavior that assists with going forward.

Being self-reliant, we know that patience is key. Patience evokes kindness to self and spills over to other areas. Handling any hard road of the unknown is not best faced with terror, anger or hate but with patience.

Can't make anything go faster or change what the test results will say. When will the doctor call us? Did the estimator do the right thing? It is patience with the unknown that will give you more energy and sense of well-being.

Preparation really helps us develop patience. We don't know the next event or when the next phone call will come saying, "We're sending your mother out." Which meant, of course, something is wrong, in a bad way. This is a call that I would get from her facility, letting me know she was on the way to the local hospital's Emergency Room.

From history I knew I had a half an hour before I had to leave my home to be in time to meet the ambulance arriving with my mom at the ER. I had by the door her notebook and "go bag." With the time I had, I left food for the cat, prayers were said and out the door to face what was next. Accepting what, I had no idea at times. I had to be patient. I had to be centered to be able to listen and evaluate what this latest event entailed.

It is impossible to prepare for everything life throws our way. The words "I wasn't prepared for this!" are said. All the planning in the world will not stop what has happened to us. Many of us are very good during the crisis and fall apart after. Nothing wrong with that. To sit and have that big cry is healing. The falling apart gives a person a chance to rebuild for the best. We want our old life back, of course we do, but that may not be an option. We make decisions that we never even thought would need to be made. We slowly build the new normal.

Always our choice. Remember when we allow OTHER people to choose our course of aid, we will never heal as well. When others choose for us, we are giving up our self-reliance and our self-determination. What others think fit for us may not be the best for us. Being self-reliant, we face ourselves and ask, "What do WE do?" "What do WE need?" We prepare as best we can in our own way. Our choice.

Self-reliance does not mean we are "Super Beings" not needing others. We know ourselves so well, we know when to ask for help. We know what kind of help we need and who we ask for that kind of assistance.

We are given every day a new opportunity on how we react to what we have been given. We attempt to be a bit prepared for all of it. What is done in the present will determine our futures.

Self-reliance comes down to you. Self-reliance is self-awareness. You sort it out, figure it out, find it, grow it, nurture it, recognize what needs adjusting and adjust it, and proceed your own way. All about what makes you well and centered. If you are uncomfortable with your circumstances presently, all you need to do is think, "From here I choose better."

From here on out, we prepare for what is best for ourselves and not despair.

9

Kindness

As we maintain our self-reliance by keeping to the basics, choosing to set aside worry, living in the present, not taking the bait, accepting what is, and preparing daily for the good, we recognize every reaction to any situation comes down to our own personal choice. So, if our welfare depends on our personal choices, let us choose kindness.

Let me say there is a big difference between being kind and being nice. Nice is a crumb, kind is the bakery. Nice is a kindergarten play, kind is the award-winning classic. One can be nice and not be kind.

You can be nice by doing something good, but nice seems always to be looking for approval. A person who continually tells you all they do that is good is being "nice." They are looking for your approval of their actions. Kindness does not look for approval from anyone.

Being kind is a state of mind that never looks for applause. Kindness is often unseen. Dropping off food, books, magazines, gifts cards to someone in need. Never letting on it is you. Doing something for someone when no one is looking and you never mention it—this is an act of kindness. Picking up a piece of trash so your town is a bit cleaner. I have mentioned this before in another book: when you pick up a piece of litter and put it in the trash, this action taken without fanfare creates a chain reaction. How? When a stranger sees you and in turn does the same. Cleaner towns to a cleaner world? I hope so.

When we are kind to ourselves, this kindness reflects in all our choices, which will determine how we live our lives. We choose to lead a complicated life or to uncomplicated our lives daily. If by chance life becomes complicated, we use our tools and skills to process forward to the calm. We are always choosing to be kind or not. Kindness brings out the good in us and draws the good to us. Simply, how we treat ourselves is how life will treat us. Practice kindness. It's its own reward. Simple! Easy? NEVER.

Let me stop here before I go forward. Kindness is not a weakness. Nor is kindness a Pollyanna view of the world with a wide-eyed look of a zombie. Kindness is the wisdom which makes you peaceful daily in the face of all critics and skeptics. I couldn't possibly name all situations that we may encounter that are challenges with swamps of negativity and possible chaos. This negativity or chaos dealt with in kindness for OURSELVES assists us to move forward towards what is best for us.

We will be kind to ourselves in the present, not waiting for something or someone to change or adjust or show up so that we can be kinder to ourselves. We are kind NOW in this moment. No matter what the issue is or what drama looms, we choose self-kindness.

We are kind to ourselves by choosing positive self-care habits. For instance, that 10, 15, 20 pounds have crept back on and you just cringe. You get the full effect of weight gain when you are looking to wear something "special" to a work event or a friend's party. You can hate yourself through the attempts to fit into something that by the law of physics proves to be impossible, or you can kindly at that moment put down the donut, piece of chocolate, cookie, cake, biscuit, chip, etc. This is the discipline of kindness. We achieve a thinner, healthier self, knowing that it will take willpower to get to and keep our best weight. I write this as my extra 10 has returned yet again. GEEZ!

We choose kindness by choosing to monitor our health, be it diabetes or high blood pressure, etc. When our bodies are sending signals that something is out of whack, we take care of it. We head to the doctor when things don't feel right. When a mole looks odd or a feeling is strange in our hearts, stomachs or heads, we choose to care for it, then let it go.

We are kind when faced with betrayal or wronged by another. After the shock wears off (and it will), we know revenge and anger are not the emotions to carry for too long. They are hurtful and harmful toxins to us. To be kind we replace those emotions with some new coping kindness skills to get through. Maybe add a new form of exercise. We could run and cry, getting thinner and less heartsick as we go. We could kick a punching bag to happiness perhaps. Write out our toxic feelings and then destroy the copy. Do something to soothe the emotional pain. Meditate, breathing exercises and choose joy, not hate.

We are kind to ourselves when we reinvent ourselves from what is, to what will be better. Reinvention of self is a constant, to reinvent our lives as the many stages and surprises of life happen. When we lose a loved one, when we lose a job, when we are a caretaker, when we lose through disasters. When our health wanes, we are forced to reinvent. What we thought once defined us may not be there anymore. Again, the job, marriage, income security or good health may vanish. As we adapt, we make new life choices.

As self-reliant beings, we may use our self-kindness to choose to move at a snail's pace and not rush to what is next. By slowing down, we let the world outside ourselves offer some solutions to contemplate. There is this quiet patience to kindness. Wisdom cannot be rushed.

Keep self-kindness when times are not right and life is unbalanced. We choose to not pout nor wail but to stand strong. We then will get on with it, fueled with the hope and concrete knowledge that one step forward may be better than sinking or going backwards. The timing of the steps may not be in our time frame but put upon us by circumstance. Why did this happen? A situation placed in our path. Now the challenge is we will go around it, under it or through it. We choose the best way possible to proceed and at our own speed.

How we best spend our time and with whom is another effective path to self-kindness. I am a big believer in the many benefits of hobbies for so many reasons. Hobbies do not judge nor are they draining. They beget joy and calm and eliminate boredom. They strike a creative spark within us. Hobbies will refocus your attention in a positive direction. Some hobbies are done with others; thus they offer socialization. Get a hobby, reach out to volunteer, to help, or join in. There are no less than a million hobbies just waiting for you to try. There are hobbies at every economic scale with all different time commitments. There are hobbies for all age groups. When the dearest of friends and I see or hear of someone trying to get into someone else's business, we shout loudly, "GET A HOBBY!" We know those who make other people's business their business is their "hobby." We don't want that or want to be that.

Volunteering can be a hobby. Someone somewhere needs you. Someone needs your talents. You say you don't have any special talents? Many volunteering situations do not need special talents. Again, there are numerous areas to volunteer. You choose. You find you don't care for the place or people? Choose again. There is some group that needs you and they need you now. Hobbies and volunteering are being kind to yourself. To learn something new to reach out to others to help is kind. I love the saying, "It costs nothing to be kind." This is correct.

And if the "Left-Handed Hiccupper Club" is not a fit after you tried it, stop and research another group after you retire the hiccup t-shirt. Who knows what you may find? It is your choice to try, reach out, gather and be open to alternatives. I couldn't list where you might fit. I do know the list would be so long you couldn't attempt everything in one lifetime. So go out and join the Antique Brick Club or Cactus Lovers of America. They are waiting for you.

We find ways to "treat" ourselves with kindness. Most valued treats do not take a lot of money or any at all. We continue to find what works and what needs to be dismissed. If finding that 10 minutes a day reading something positive works for you, then do it. If you find cooking feeds your soul or gardening or sports or movies, do that. That little kindness you do for yourself will create the best for you.

Choose to find five minutes a day to sit quietly to feel the peace to get to the center of the issue, situation, future dreams or plans. Treat yourself well by saving a dollar or more a day towards creation of wealth building. Your choice, your treat. No great future comes without the preparedness now.

Take that first walk around the block to gain a new healthy habit of daily exercise. Just take one step, one new gentle yoga class, one less cookie or chip, one thank-you to another, one hello to meet a new friend.

Small actions done daily or frequently lead to the new and improved you. This is gently crafting self-reliance.

Being kind to ourselves enables us to stay strong through the next phone call, email, letter or text that brings another level of uneasiness our way. We will stand, take a deep breath and be kind to ourselves. Also, being kind to ourselves means we choose not to lose ourselves in addictions, be it drugs, gambling, over-shopping, alcohol, food or any other addiction. Addictions bring hangovers that take our time to get back to center. We want to skip having to fight to get back to being centered in our awareness.

We can also get addicted to feeling bad, feeling hopeless or depressed. Bottom-line addictions dull us. We are not present to see what is coming or deal with what has arrived, and we may miss the direction to our next new opportunity. If you are a caretaker, you do not have the luxury to be deluded because we are always on call, always driving somewhere or having to make some important decision for another. We need to stay clear and watch and listen for the next best action.

You may receive, in the middle of an issue, a "fool's" call, giving unsolicited advice. We may want to scream, "Do you think I am dumb and haven't thought of what you are suggesting?" No, we let the fools be. They will always be around. Some are well-intentioned and others are just plain annoying. You know the difference. Breathe deep. They are only a test to see how well you are handling being kind to yourself. You half-listen as they are go on and on. You can answer with one word, "Really?" and off the phone. We know they will call again. Kindness is spending less time with them or no time at all. Again, it's your choice.

What is a fool? Someone who just talks off the top of their head, giving advice without the history or knowledge of your reality. We all know them and sometimes we may have been one.

When we sense a discomfort from another person, place or situation, it should raise a red flag. As those red flags wave, we know it's time to pay attention and sort out what has been presented. Was that a lie I just heard? Was that a new ache in a place I should not have an ache? Is that red flag a signal of change ahead?

No need to be in a place or with a person that makes you uncomfortable. Sometimes later you may get the answer and find out your intuition saved you from something really unpleasant. Always paying attention to your intuition is one of the self-cares of kindness. Do not place or leave yourself in anything that is unkind to you when your gut is screaming something is not right.

We recognize when things get "ugly." As an example, our medical system can be a complicated challenge to navigate, whether for yourself or as a caretaker for another. You can become somewhat frazzled trying to determine what has been done, what should be done or what is being done. When things get uglier still, you may loop day in/day out on all the doings or what was not done at all.

As you are leaving your person in a medical facility, you check things. To check that the tasks WERE done today. Not letting anything remain undone so that the tasks spill into tomorrow, adding to tomorrow's trials.

This is a mix of self-awareness, of being in the present, self-reliant to get something done and being kind to oneself so you can delete any later anguish that arises that you left something undone.

This is carrying out that last intuitive thought. "Did I check that the water pitcher is filled?" "Did I check that the call bell was in reach when I left my person?" That is kindness for them and you. Self-reliance breeds a peace of mind. How? We trust ourselves to listen to our intuition and proceed accordingly. This is self-reliance. We lovingly accept and do what we know is best.

Self-reliance is about building our strength and valuing ourselves through action, word and deed. Self-reliance is not settling for second best, but if that is the option at any given time, we accept what is. We recognize that healing, mending and learning take time and effort to create the new from the now. We are kind with ourselves about the timing of such.

When we are self-reliant, we practice being people of our word. We nurture our integrity and value our own worth. We live by example in words and deeds. We do not plan tasks we cannot complete. We do not make commitments of our time we cannot keep—in work and play. We do not over-extend or over-promise. We are the keepers of our word. As keepers of our word, we trust ourselves to not cause any hurt for another insofar as we are able.

And just when everything is calm and you are in a very good place with the world, the phone rings and the message comes you are up to bat to handle a new situation. We know the time spent with this new challenge will pass. So, we will handle it with some new tools to keep us centered and self-directed. We have learned to endure, conquer, overcome the past challenges and have proceeded to the new. We don't have to like it, but we accept what is happening. To grow, to find, to learn, to be at, to meet, to be in, to be with or to be without. We learn and honor the multiple lessons that come in a lifetime.

We become centered in the faith of completion, faith of resolve, faith of assistance, faith of the unknown to the known. We thank those who have assisted us moving forward. We practice gratitude for the process of faith. We maintain our faith, knowing trials will work out over and over and over.

We may have to look hard in the struggle to find a place of peace to keep us going, to keep us clear, to keep us healthy. Bottom line: we ALWAYS control our place of peace; nothing outside us does. Our peace becomes unbalanced when we allow outside situations make us angry, upset or confused.

By building our kindness, we choose what works to move us towards peace. This differs for each of us. On some days nothing seems to work. We have faith that tomorrow will bring answers and a new plan of action.

Self-reliance is being self-aware. Being self-actualized means you get it daily. We recognize what robs us of being clear.

Knowing the difference between what is good for us and what to stay away from. Knowing if you choose knowingly to sit with what may not be the right thing, we create a possible negative consequence. We know we will be kind to ourselves as we face and handle such consequences.

I have spoken in the past of walking your worth for self-confidence (Attitude!). Now we practice standing our strength. Now we stand strong in our self-reliance. Let's practice. Stand up, both feet planted, no sagging knees. Shoulders back. Head up. Arms at your sides. Chin up. Eyes looking forward, not down. We STAND strong. We will practice standing straight and strong at the grocery store, at work, at the post office and church. We practice the feeling that whatever is happening, we have accepted it and we will get through it. Daily we have the chance to choose to get it right NOW in the moment. We recognize this and choose kindness for ourselves.

I wish us all to STAND strong as we kindly choose to be self-reliant.

About the Author

Karen Okulicz is also the author of "Try! A Survival Guide to Unemployment!"; "Decide! How to make any Decision" and "Attitude! For your best lived Life."

The books are utilized resources in workforce development programs. They have an honored placement on the Self-Publishing Hall of Fame.

Ms. Okulicz continues to be an invited speaker on her book topics. She has hosted and produced the radio show "Workline."

She lives "down the shore" in New Jersey.

ORDER FORM

Order online www.GUIDESFORYOU.com or fax to 732-681-1318
Mail: Checks payable to K-Slaw, Inc., P.O. Box 375, Belmar, NJ 07719

	Amount	Price	Total
"Try!" A Survival Guide to Unemployment	_____	X _____	_____
ISBN# 978-09644260-0-9			
"Decide!" How to make any Decision	_____	X _____	_____
ISBN# 978-09644260-1-6			
"Attitude!" For your best lived life	_____	X _____	_____
ISBN# 978-09644260-2-3			
"Stand!" Choosing to be Self-Reliant	_____	X _____	_____
ISBN# 978-0-9644260-3-0			

Please add 7% Tax for NJ only _____

Shipping $15.00 per box of 100 books   Shipping and Handling _____

Purchase order #_____   TOTAL _____

Bulk Discount 1-10 $10.00 per book, 11 to 99 $6.00 per book, 100 to 999 $5.00 per book,
1000 to 4,999 $3.00 per book and over 5,000 $2.50 per book.
Books can be mixed for the best discount!

Call 1-888-529-6090 • Fax 732-681-1318 • Email Karen@guidesforyou.com
Visa and Mastercard Accepted.
eBooks available on website: www.GUIDESFORYOU.com

Ship to: Name _____ Title _____

Organization _____

Address _____

City _____ State _____ ZIP _____

Phone# _____ Fax _____

Email _____

TAX ID# 223325968

THANK YOU!

Made in the USA
Middletown, DE
19 May 2021

40087271R00189